First published in 2025
by Liston and Jones

Text and Illustrations © Daniel Jones 2025

All rights reserved

Typography:
Atma, Sylexiad

While the characters at the start of the book are made up, the characters at the end are people in other countries who have suffered in different ways for following Jesus. Their stories are all taken from Open Doors, and you can find out more on their website at:

www.opendoors.org
www.opendoorsuk.org

For other books I've written or illustrated, visit:
www.anchor-lines.com

In Billy's house, children help wash up the dishes, and yesterday Billy had washed a whole heap,

but Billy's big brother has broken his finger, and Billy's now stuck doing dishes all week.

Now normally Billy
is peaceful and patient...

... but seeing his brother
relaxed on a chair,
while he's busy cleaning...

... he's suddenly angry!

And Billy shouts out from the sink,

IT'S NOT FAIR!

Chris has been grounded
for breaking a window.
It wasn't him –
but his mum found him there.

Sue's in detention – she's missed out on lunchtime for filling the teacher's new handbag with glue.

She'd done it – but so had Jo, Jasmine and Jenna!
They'd all four been bad but they'd only caught Sue.

Now Sue's in trouble and feeling frustrated.
She's stuck inside and her friends, they don't care!
She looks through the window
– they're free in the sunshine!

Noah's been told that he can't go to football

A party's on – noone's invited poor Claire

Becky's been bullied

and Jack's lost his job

And all of them cry,

IT'S NOT FAIR!

Paul's been imprisoned
for telling a story,
a story he wanted
and needed to share.
He's broken no laws
but he's shut up indoors.

And what did Paul say?

He told them the truth and he told them of Jesus.
He spoke of God's hope and his justice and care.
Paul was content to be following Jesus
And never **once** said, "It's not fair"

See, Jesus was punished for things he'd not done.
They lifted him up on a cross in the air.

And though it was awful, he did it for us.
"Father, not my will, but yours" was his prayer

Jesus was innocent – we deserved punishment.
That's what would really have truly been fair.
But that's not what I want – I'm so glad for Jesus,
and this is the good news we share.

Many love Jesus and call him their master.
Sometimes they're treated in ways that aren't fair,
like Leah, who's captured and kept far away
from her friends and her family's care.

Or Joo Min who bravely went back to her country though Christians are in so much danger out there, to take this good news to the people who need it instead of her staying in safety elsewhere.

Or those in Iran who must meet up in secret
for teaching and stories and help and for prayer.
Like Moshen and Simin, they'd rather have Jesus
than give up and cry, 'it's not fair!'

So pray for your brothers and sisters who suffer.
Your words make a difference, you'll help them to bear
the challenge of being God's daughters and sons
in a world that seems sometimes unfair.

For those who love Jesus – it may mean we suffer,
and though you feel lonely or nervous or scared,
if You trust your saviour and do what he tells you,
king Jesus will be with you there.

Things really do feel unfair at times, and sometimes what we need most is just to know that someone understands – to listen, give us a hug, to show us that they care (even if we're overreacting!)

But God also wants to gives us a bigger perspective. First, he shows us what an amazing gift we've been given. It really wasn't fair for Jesus to die in our place – but for those who know him, it's the most wonderful gift you could imagine. It's a source of joy that can make a difference to even the roughest days.

Second, he reminds us that even though we matter deeply to him, our lives aren't the only ones that matter. There are others suffering what looks like awful unfairness because of their faith in Jesus, and we can make a real difference in their lives simply by remembering them and praying for them.

So don't make light of the unfairness others experience – even if it might seem small. But don't let it be the only unfairness they know about.

Some of the stories in this poem – Anna, Joo Min, Moshen and Simin – are taken from Open Doors, a charity that helps support the persecuted church, and makes resources to help us to pray for and give to our brothers and sisters around the world. You can find out more at:

www.opendoors.org
www.opendoorsuk.org

"Blessed are those who are persecuted because of righteousness,
for theirs is the kingdom of heaven."
Matthew 5:10

"And pray in the Spirit on all occasions with all kinds of prayers and requests. With this in mind, be alert and always keep on praying for all the Lord's people."
Ephesians 6:18

www.ingramcontent.com/pod-product-compliance
Lightning Source LLC
Chambersburg PA
CBHW041125070526
44584CB00003B/277